Divine Discoveries in History and the Arts

Music, Dance and Spirituality in the Arts, Maria Theresa Duncan

PAMELA DE FINA

Balboa Press books may be ordered through booksellers or by contacting:

Balboa Press
A Division of Hay House
1663 Liberty Drive
Bloomington, IN 47403
www.balboapress.com
844-682-1282

ISBN: 978-1-9822-6088-0 (sc)
ISBN: 978-1-9822-6090-3 (hc)
ISBN: 978-1-9822-6089-7 (e)

Library of Congress Control Number: 2020925649

Print information available on the last page.

Balboa Press rev. date: 09/09/2021

Contents

The Relationship Between Music and Dance

La Belle Epoch

Dedicated to: My Father, Joseph, whom I always felt elevated to a Divine level of Light, Peace and Love.

Beethoven Symphony No.7 in A Major- Allegretto

The Divine Message in this Musical Composition by Beethoven, is that it has been said that the Allegretto, is the embodiment of the Seven Gifts of the Holy Spirit, being-Wisdom, Understanding, Counsel, Fortitude, Knowledge, Piety and Fear of the Lord, and I have found this to be true! The Music is a living, breathing, witness to the Spirit, in movement. St. Bernard has said that the Spirit illumines the Mind, and instills an attraction to the Divine. Understanding, is a view taken by the Mind, while the former is an experience undergone by the Heart, one is Light, and one is Love, as they unite and complete one another. A Wise and loving Heart is Understanding. Understanding helps one relate all Truths to a Supernatural purpose, because the music is felt from within the heart and soul, and expressed outward and upward in Praise and in Union with the Glory and Majesty of God ! It is a Prayer in motion and becomes a dance because of the music. Music is felt in the heart, and the gestures respond to the music. Theresa said during our practices," This is your dance, the light soul leading the darker shades of the soul towards the light". Thirty-five years later, I am still learning, and growing Spiritually, through the Music and the Dance! It has been a Salvation during the Corona Virus- Confinement. Each time I repeat it, new Revelations of the Spirit within me come to Light, as I become more aware of the intrinsic Spiritual meaning. I am transformed by the Music from within. It is a true and living Prayer in motion! In the book, edited by Katherine Teck, Making Music for Modern Dance, published by Oxford University Press, "Dancing to Beethoven Seventh Symphony Allegretto", she mentions the open air performance that I was filmed in at the Trianon Palace, in Versailles France. I was very honored and humbled to read this, I remembered what Theresa said while she was teaching me, as her soft words, had become a part of my soul. She compares the Choreography, as being very similar to Isadora Duncan, whom was the first Artist to dance to this music. This film can be seen at the Jerome Robbins Library at Lincoln Center in New York City. Isadora Duncan said that she was not a Dancer, and that all of her life she only listened to Music, which is it's Rhythm, Soul, and Harmony, of the very Life of Dance. Plato in his Republic, states, that the study of music is necessary for the balance and health of mankind. Music brings us Beauty and Life. Isadora's idea was a Spiritual one, as she said, place your hand on your heart and listen to your soul, and you will know what to do. She said if she were only a Dancer, she would not speak, but that she was a Teacher with a Mission.

I am continually mystified by the living spirit in the music and the gestures. Why, I ask, at this time of the Global Pandemic and Confinement, do we refer more to the Holy Spirit? For me, the Spirit has inspired me to move to this Music. It is the Composer, Beethoven, who was inspired, because the Holy Spirit is very much alive in the Musical Phrases. It's through, Prayer, Meditation, Scripture, Art, and Music, that our Minds and Hearts are lifted upward towards God, which restores our equilibrium, and direction in life, leading us into a more intimate relationship with Him! The experience I had with Theresa, in learning the dances to the great music of Beethoven, Chopin, Liszt and others, did not replace my Faith, but deepened it, being a part of my own, unique Spiritual Journey, an integral part of my own sufferings, healing, and transformations.

Maria Theresa who was named Wind Fire in one of her photos taken by Edward Steichen on the Acropolis, was inspired by the same Spirit, as she said she danced the Sacred Fire!

Theresa was celebrated as the greatest Musical Dramatist of her day! Theresa stated that Isadora's Art could not explained, and was not a system of steps, but a deep working of the Universe, and a profound vision to see with an inner vision, the progression of Musical figures in the development of a Composition, in harmony with the Music! Theresa stated: " I as a Dancer have always approached Isadora's Art from a Musical-Dramatic side-I wish to transmit the Drama into the minds and hearts of the audience." This won her the applaud of both Crirics and the public at Carnegie Hall, Theatre de Champs Elysees, Berlin, Vienna, Budapest, and many more Cultural Institutions, University's and Theatres, worldwide.

Theresa founded her own Group of Dancers called the HELICONIADES in 1930, New York City, of which Kay Bardsley was a member. The Dancers were of Greek origin, but born in the United States, and were singing and dancing to Poetry dating back to Antiquity! They were given a thorough training by Theresa lasting one and a half years, in Music, Dance and the Fine Arts before performing. Theresa's deepest regret is that she did not remain in Athens to direct the School that Isadora Duncan had promised. She said that after Isadora had wined and dined her, she abruptly changed her plans, and they all had to leave, without a reason.

While I was residing in Versailles, I found a Greek Mythological Statue in the Gardens, that reminded me very much of Maria Theresa Duncan, and the manner in which she draped the Cape on her body which was an integral part of the Dance, and in her facial expression, serious and deep. Theresa was an intensely, dramatic Artist, who integrated Music, Drama, Art, Painting and Sculpting, Philosophy, and Poetry, as had been celebrated in Ancient Greece in Delphi by Apollo and the Muses!

Delphino

After the death of my Father in 1987, as well as Maria Theresa Duncan, the same year, my world was turned upside down. I was truly protected by my Father, and she in the dance world. My Father was so supportive and said to me" You are meant to represent Theresa," She has been very generous to you! I left New York City where I had been residing, at East Seventy-Fourth Street, for nearly twenty years, after living in Santa Barbara, California where I attended UCSB, Graduate and Undergraduate in Art History, before being accepted and attending Villa Schifanoia,in Fiesole, Florence, Italy, Graduate School of Fine Arts, M.A. Art History. I was married to Andre Andreoli, an Artist and traveling to Europe, where he was showing his Paintings, in International Art Gallery's. He always sold all of his Paintings and to many celebrities.

I was intuitively guided to reside in Versailles. I was unaware of the discoveries I would find there. As my Father once said to me before I was leaving for Switzerland, "Now, what discoveries will you make this time?" He was always my closest confidant and best friend aside from being a wonderful and most devoted and loving Father. He understood me totally. I was a completely, Fathers- Daughter!

I loved Versailles, and spent nearly every day, between the Gardens, the Chateau, and researching my family name and history in the Library. I was fascinated, by the beautiful Ancient Texts, and found a very rich History, written in Latin and Ancient French. Thanks to the generosity of the Library, I was able to discover the origins of the name De Fina, with a dauphin on the Blaison or (Crest), as my Fathers has. Dauphin, in Latin is – Delphinus,which recalls the ancient city in Greece, Phocide, origins of the Allobroge race, the first Ancsestors of the Dauphinoise territory, which extended from Milan to Vienne and Lyon, to Geneva Switzerland. Patria Delphinatus-" Dauphine." Apollo Delphinios, was adored in the 6 c. B.C. at Delphes,in the form of a Dolphin, on the island of Delphi. The founders of the first race of Dauphins, originated from a Venetian family Delfino. The ancient name for the territory- Dauphinoise, was Le Viennois, which became Le Vienne., derived from Venice, the Italian Republic. The real meaning of the Word-Symbol, "Dauphin" is Christian . Beginning in Ancient times, it began to prefigure the character of Christ the Savior-Fisher of men. The Dolphin, and Fish, (Poisson), was a friend of fishermen, and celebrated by, Esope, Herodote, Pollien, and honored in the Greek, Etruscan and Galois temples. The image of the dauphin-poisson or (dolphin-fish,) has been since the beginning of Ancient times a Christian symbol linked to Christ, the Guide, and Savior of Marines Expeditions . Christ is the Guide and Savior of all Mankind. The Dolphin lives in water and nourishes the people. After having researched extensively in Versailles, I decided to visit the Ancient Territory Dauphine. I first went to Uriage-les-Bains, near Grenoble, and the Monastery of Chartreuse. Afterwards, I was intuitively guided by an inner voice, to go to Abbaye St. Antoine, a Medieval Village where the Knights of St. Antoine, the Egyptian Hermit of the Desert, who was the Founder of Monasticism in the East, and built Monasteries and Hospitals, to heal the sick and dying, of which, one still remains there. His Relics were brought there by a French Noble Woman. I had in my possession my Fathers Crest or(Blaison.) Blue and Gold with a dauphin en chef nageant au naturel. I was introduced to Gisele Bricault, author of-" Un Décor Pour L'Histoire Dauphinoise," and other books, an expert on Dauphine, who after consulting with the Conseil Delphinal, called me and told me that yes, your Fathers Crest-(Blaison), is a big thing, and you can find it, registered in J. B Reipstap, under Fino (da). " D'Or a' la Fasce d' azur, soutenue d'un demi pal de meme, le taut accompanied by a dauphin en chef nageant au naturel." She had consulted with Le Conseil Delphinal! The dauphin en chef was originally attributed to High Government and Religious Officials. The Order of Military and Religious Knights. The TAU in Blue Azur was the Symbol of the Cross, and placed on their Religious cloaks, worn by the Knights, as a cross of blue enamel laced with gold. This was their sign of distinction as an order of Hospitaliers Antonins,of the Middle Ages in the XII century. Most of the Da Fino line originated from Milan, which was also Dauphine in the year 1000 A.D. It was originally an independent ancient, Medieval Province ruled by the Dauphins or the Princes that carried the title of Dauphin, and the Symbol on the Blaison.(Crest) It was the Symbol of Christ the Savior, as well as a title of Nobility. This race ruled for 300 years, between 900 until 1349 A.D, when it was sold to King Phillipe De Valois of France by Humberto II Dalphino, of whom it is said he was relate to.. The Princes of the Sons of the Kings of France were the only ones given the name and title of Dauphin. In LaRousse Encyclopedia- DeFina, is from Province. I am not going into a detailed chronology at this time, I will elaborate on this history later in another book.

The Justice System- LIBERATES DALPHINAT-JUDICEM appellationum DALPHINATUS.

The Departments of the Justice, Military, were ruled by the Dauphins, who exercised their rights and laws over the territory. DAUPHINE. The creation of the Conseil DELPHINALE, and the transfer of these states to France was by Humbert II, who created a superior Justice and Finance System, which is the principal achievement of Dauphine until today. All of the judgements of the Dauphine Counsel had a coin with a DAUFIN in the middle and with this quotation printed on it: Sigillum Consilii Delphinalis. Which signified and registered the tax that had to be paid every month before the Magistrates and the Treasury. The company was under the direction of the War, Justice, and Finances. It was Humbert II who was responsible for creating the Treasury into 3 Depts. By which he later reduced to one.

The parallels between my Fathers career as Chief Justice of the Court of Tax, Department of Finance in New York City, who was responsible for the re-organization of the Department of Taxation from 3 separate departments by which he reduced to one, single Department by which all tax hearings were held, both Formal and Informal. The success of this change is written in an authentic booklet, whereby he received official recognition from the City Officials. He also wrote new laws, and made significant contributions and changes in the domains of Government, Finance and Military in NYC, and was on the UN Executive Committee.and was Host of the UN Ball. Many International Ambassadors, famous tennis players and athletes, as well as International Society were his house guests, and friends.

This discovery for me was a personal, historical and spiritual one. My Faith deepened and matured, in the region .I felt my ancient religious roots, Many of the First Religious Orders and Monastery's began there, and still flourish today. Abbaye Hautecombe, Cluny, Chartreuse. I attended a Church in Aix-les-Bains, Savoie who had a remarkable Priest, that because of his outstanding homelies my Faith became more profound. By following my own inner voice, and the path of the Dauphins, in memory of my Father, I found Christ, and a Spiritual Calling! I had a significant dream in 2001, before going to the region. I saw a gold cross on a ring like a wedding band. I visited the Abbaye Hautecombe founded by St. Bernard in the 800's, and saw the ring that I had dreamt about in their boutique. I asked what Cross is that? They replied, this is the Cross of Savoie.

A Spiritual Journey

After having studied and researched the great Renaissance Masters in Florence, Italy as Michelangelo, Leonardo Da Vinci, Botticelli, Raphael, and others, at the Graduate School of Fine Arts, Villa Schifanoia/Rosary College, now Dominican College. While studying the great Renaissance Masters in Florence, Italy, I began making observations about the body in movement through the Paintings and Sculptures . I was immersed in the Art world, and in the company of Great Artists. I worked for Art Galleries and learned the business of the Art World through an art dealer buying and selling at the famous auction houses. It was a highly creative and stimulating time in my life, for this was my Passion, the Art and the History of the Lives of Artists. I moved to Manhattan New York, to have a career in the Art world, and returned to the Harkness House of Ballet to continue the dance. I was intuitively led to seek the dance of Isadora Duncan, although I had never seen it before, except in a film; I felt that it expressed the works of Art, that I had studied in Florence. After two years of searching, I found Theresa Duncan. She was a Musical Genius, who choreographed many works of her own, and was celebrated internationally as a Solo, Musical Dramatist. I discovered that the Masterpieces, that I had studied in Florence as Sandro Botticelli, La PrimaVera, Le Printemp. The Allegory of Spring was the same painting that Isadora Duncan created dances to while visiting Florence in 1905. Theresa chose me for her group called the Maria Theresa Heritage Group, as she said I understood the Art of the Isadorian Dance, because I had studied the great works of Art in Florence, Italy, and which were an integral part of the Dance of Isadora. I presented lectures revealing the inter-relation, and parallels between the Painters, Sculptures of the Renaissance, Greek and Roman and the Dance of Isadora . The Paintings and Sculptures came to life through the Classical music of Chopin, Beethoven, Bach, Liszt and others. It was Art coming to Life! I lectured, taught and performed, in France, New York, Florida, California, beginning with the United Nations in 1979, the Sorbonne University, Paris, 1984, Santa Barbara City College Abroad Program, The House of the Redeemer, New York City, Graymoor- Fransiscan Friary, Ancient Orchesis Study Group, Athens, Greece. Trianon Palace, Versailles- Film- Jerome Robbins Library, New York City.

Versailles Calling!

The death of My Father Joseph George De Fina and Maria Theresa Duncan, both came as a shock to me, and at the same time, and just a few months apart! My Father was my most cherished and loved best friend and confidant. I had a True Family who were always there for me, positive, loving, and with unconditional support. I was extremely fortunate and Blessed. I desired to do everything I could to keep their Legacy alive, as they had both been so generous. My Father had been there with me the whole time I knew Maria Theresa and was very supportive and understanding. When they died, my life was turned upside down. I no longer had my two great protectors, one in my Family, and the other in the Dance World. Before leaving New York City, I presented a recital-lecture, at the House of the Redeemer, a Renaissance Villa, and Historical Landmark in the heart of New York City. The Library was originally at the Ducal Palace in the 16century, just outside of Urbino, Italy. I was so moved by the Beauty of the Library, and the Wood, which was transported on a boat by Edith Shephard Fabbri and her husband Count Ernesto Fabbri, of Urbino, at the outbreak of World War 1. The Wood was genuine, and I felt extremely peaceful, and at home there. I presented a Lecture- Concert there which is an ideal place!

After leaving New York City, I was intuitively guided to reside in Versailles. I was unaware of the discoveries I would find there, and what a rich and positive phase in my life it would be. I lived not far from the Chateau, where I frequented daily, the Gardens, the Library, where I did extensive genealogical research on my Family name. I felt completely in Balance with the Universe. The Chateau and Gardens radiated positive, Solar energy. The Gardens, aligned with Greek and Roman Mythological Statues, formed a perfect harmony and Balance with the Solar reflections, created by le Roi Soleil, and Andre Le Notre, who designed the Gardens. I taught Ateliers de Dance in Paris, and brought students to Dance in the Gardens, with the consent from the Chateau. I was so inspired by the Music of Jean-Baptiste Lully, the Musician for, Le Roi Soleil, Louis XIV, that I created a movement to "The Ballet Music for the Roi Soleil " of which I taught to the students and still practice today at my own home in Palm Beach Gardens, during the confinement, and has been so healing and inspiring! They are Eternal Treasures, and Melodies of the Heart and Soul. I practiced the choreography of the Beethoven Symphony #7, Allegretto, and was able to reconstruct the version that Theresa had originally taught me, by remembering her words, and the gestures came naturally. This was filmed at the Trianon Palace, and can be seen at the Jerome Robbins Library in New York City. It was an ideal place for the Arts, Music, Drama and Dance. Western European Culture reached an Apex in Versailles, as Nature, Greek and Roman Statuary, Renaissance Art, Architecture, Music, form a happy Celestial Union.

Maria Theresa always said" The dances are Spiritual, but we don't talk about it." Certainly, the dances she taught me were living prayers in motion. The Beethoven, which she said was "Your Dance," the Light Soul leading the Darker shades of the Soul towards the Light." A Call to follow the Light, towards a greater union with Jesus Christ. This is a lifelong journey. The movements of the Dance ascend from Heavy to Light, in rhythm with the music, originating from the heart . The dance has become more profound with time. It was a beautiful gift from Theresa to teach me. She was a very gentle, deep, humane and generous person. I was always uplifted to a more serene, and divinely happy level in her presence. After my traveling days came to a screeching halt, because I became sick with advanced breast cancer and moved home, to Palm Beach, where I had grown up. My Mother Josephine and sister Angela, helped me throughout this difficult time, and I am forever grateful for them! I have always had a very loving relationship with my sister, She has always been there for me in times of need, and I for her !

I had been given a Cross to endure, and my previous life and experiences, had well prepared me for this phase. The dance became an integral part of my own sufferings, and source of Healing, deepening my relationship with God through the Music. The music of the Allegretto awakens in the Heart the Spirit, and the gestures respond naturally. Theresa always said," It takes a great Soul to dance to great Music, anyone can do pretty little dances, but this was something entirely apart from learning steps and physical precision. My prayers and reading the Gospels, homelies and Lives of the Saints, Religious Sisters and Priests were my most sure path to healing.

Gardens of the Chateau of Versailles, photo credit-P. de Fina Mythological statue, that reminded
me of Maria Theresa, and the manner in which she draped the cape on her body. There was
a very precise way of positioning the cape which was an integral part of the dance. Theresa
was a very serious and dramatic artist-dancer, whom integrated music, drama and art in
her creative masterpieces. To be in her presence was like being in the presence of a living,
breathing work of art. There, I understood the art of Maria Theresa on a very deep level.

"Apollo with Lyre on two Dolphins", Les Jardins du Chateau de Versailles, Gardens of the Chateau of Versailles. Photo credit-P.amela de Fina

Les Jardins du Chateau de Versailles, designed by Le Notre, under Le Roisoleil- photo credit-Pamela de Fina

After Theresa and my Father died in 1987, I resided in Versailles, and taught ateliers de Danse at the Centre de Danse du Marais in Paris, and brought the students to dance in the Gardens., which was an ideal place, as Theresa had often spoken about.. There, I discovered the same philosophy and elements, of the dance, were present in the gardens.. The mythological statues, nature, music, and the perfect design of the gardens in harmony, with the solar reflections. "I found many parallels between the gardens and the dance, where, Art, Music, and Nature form a Happy Celestial Union.

"Fountain of Apollo", designed by Le Brun, sculpted by Jean Baptiste Tubi, a Roman in the King's service between-1668-1670. Photo credit-Pamela de Fina

Villa Schifanoia-
Florence Italy

I was accepted as a full time Graduate student in the MA. Art History, at the VILLA SHIFANOIA, Graduate Program in Art History in Florence, Fiesole, Italy. The Villa was originally purchased by an American Ambassador for the Vatican under the reign of Pope Pious XII. Upon his death he left it to the Vatican to be used for Graduate Studies in the Arts, then Rosary College, and now the Dominican. Rosary College and Harvard University students researched at the Villa I Tatti, Bernard Berenson Renaissance Study Center. Pope Pious VI was the residing Pope at the time. 1975-6. My Father who loved Italy, and whose Parents, Rose and Rocco, immigrated from Rome to New York in the late 1800's, decided to take my sister and I on a trip to Florence together, and we stayed at the PENSIONA TOURNABUONI BEACCI. He and Signorina BEACCI engaged in many enjoyable conversations reminiscing about mutual friends and places. My Father had spent many years in Italy, both coaching the Italian Davis and French Davis Cup Players, as well as being on the UN Executive Committee, and was much loved and admired by his European friends He said that upon visiting Portofino, they asked him to become Mayor, he declined saying he didn't like politics. According to many sources, as Family name Research Center found that our name originated from the Tuscany region, records dating back to 1122, show the name FINUS, that became FINO, FINI and FINA and other variants taken from the pet name of Delphinus Fino . The Archives show evidence of a family with the surname da FINO-which was registered in Milan, in J. P. REIPSTAP. This crest is my Father's -De Fina. There are also records of a Fini family whose members settled in Venice in 1571 after fleeing the Island of Cyprus, when it came under Turkish rule. Greek-Roman origans. According to one anscestry. 12% of my DNA is from Greece and Cyprus. 83 % is from San Marino, Lazio Region, Vatican City, Rome, and others, which keeps changing, Initially, primarily, Greece and Italy, but also found in France and Switzerland, In Larousse Encyclopedia– De Fina, is from the Province and surrounding territory, written in Latin. In 1649 members of this family were admitted to Venetian Royal Society. The personal name Fina became popular in Tuscany because of the devotion to the Saint Fina or Serafina. She was from San Gimignano, near Sienna, where she died in 1263 at the age of 15. She is venerated throughout the region, and in San Gimignano a chapel was constructed in the 15th century, in her honor. It is also curious to note that the Italian word" Serafino", means, "Seraph", which according to Christian theology is a member of the highest Ordre of Angels, above the Cherubim.

Masterpieces by Raphael in Rome- HUMANISM IN THE RENAISSANCE. 1508-1511.

In the Popes Study- La Stanza DELLA SEGNATURA - Three Paintings reflecting the affinity between Christianism and the wisdom of Antiquity, face one another and reveal an accord, both in subject matter and elements that correspond to one another.

Parnassus- Apollo is shown playing a musical instrument looking upward to the sky, as Poetry was celebrated as the highest faculty of the Spirit! Apollo and the muses, are surrounded by ancient and modern Poets depicting a harmonious accord between the Classical and Christian Humanist Worlds.
The School of Athens, Raphael, 1508-11 Stanza Della SEGNATURA-Vatican Palaces- The architecture represents 16 century Roman style, in a Greek Cross design reminiscent of ancient Basilicas. Plato and Aristotle standing in the center, represent the two schools of thought, Ancient and Renaissance. They appear to be moving slowly forward in harmony. Plato is pointing his finger upward towards the realm of ideas, while Aristotle represents the earthy dimension of the earth as his hand is lifted forward and downward. They are surrounded by famous philosophers, thinkers and men of letters, that appear to unite under the Archway, symbolizing a coming together of the ancient and Renaissance worlds.

Disputation of the Sacrament- Raphael-1508-11- STANZA DELLA SEGNATURA,

On the Altar in the Center is the HOST, and representing Christ, and is the focus of the three levels, of the Church. The bottom layer represents the Militant Church, with Laity and Religious. The Upper layer depicts The Divine Trinity, Virgin Mary, and St. John.

The three Paintings are facing one another revealing harmony and accord between the Ancient World and the RENAISSANCE HUMANISTIC CULTURE!

Parnassus and Apollo, by Raphael, 1508-11, Rome, Vatican Palaces -Stanza Della Segnatura

Disputation on the Sacrament by Raphael, 1508-11, Vatican Palaces- Stanza Della Segnatura

The School of Athens, 1508-11-Vatican Palaces -Stanza Della Segnatura

A Divine Encounter

Maria Theresa, who shed her brilliance, love and light upon humanity for a span of 92 years. We miss her deeply and profoundly, her radiant presence, deep wisdom, her graceful, loving and gentle soul! We are now only left with her creations to keep the *flame* of her *fiery spirit* alive! Her sincere passion, her generous heart, a truly great human being who bestowed the gift of her friendship upon me for close to ten years, and who wished me to keep her *flame* burning, and I'm so deeply and humbly honored to do so, most of all in her memory! She possessed the secret power to express beauty, love, and truth, through the most noble of human gestures! To give birth to others all that was beautiful and strong! This beauty in movement only serves to the highest degree to give meaning to the human race; that is love for the past generation, for the present, and for the future one! She brought depth of feeling, naturalness, grace, spontaneity, all these qualities she possessed so completely, that coupled with an understanding of the music, was able to give birth to her own creations, as Isadora had. For when I first saw her in a Performance, I thought she was Isadora! She was so deeply moving and human. She carried the stamp of a great soul deeply connected to Classical Antiquity, and at the same time powerfully present, expressing the sorrows of the human condition––death, separation, loss, which were so much a part of Isadora's life, right up until her own untimely death. Yes, Theresa after Isadora had this same ability to create gestures that communicated the human drama of mankind, which originated from her heart and soul as Isadora had. Her dances told the story of the human condition, as did the music of the great musicians such as Franz Liszt, Chopin, Schubert, Brahms, etc. Isadora and Maria Theresa were on the same wavelength, mentally and emotionally, as the musicians, and coupled with the innate spontaneous ability to express her body through movement, created dances that were unique, original masterpieces! The dances were her own, because she created them with her entire being––that's altogether different than imitating someone's choreography. Theresa also had a brilliant career, as many of the same people that saw her dance knew Isadora and had the same reaction as I had.

As I contemplated for many years after the death of Maria Theresa Duncan, whether I should write on the subject or not, I was continually drawn back to her, and what I had experienced with her. My friendship with her lasted from 1978 until 1987, the same year my own father died, who was so understanding and supportive as I pursued this path in life which was destined to be. So it's that I feel compelled to recount my personal experiences with Theresa, an artist most similar to Isadora; who carried the same creative genius in her ability to invent dances to the great composers; and as a person, who was truly the most extraordinary person I've had the great honor of knowing. She danced from the inner awakening of her heart center, as I've seen no other dancer do. She made such a strong and deep impression on my entire being that I knew I needed to follow this mysterious path for my own salvation! As she once said during one of our practices dancing to Chopin's "Funeral March," Sonata in B minor Op. 35 which we practiced over and over until it was perfected, "Now, dear, when you feel deeply: That's life!" Theresa was radiant and electric, with a deeply human quality. People always asked me if she was my mother. The out of the ordinary events that led me to Theresa were another reminder to me that this was destiny, that life had a higher divine order or purpose for my soul. While in Paris I visited the Raymond Duncan Gallery and asked where I could find the dance of Isadora. There I was told that the most astute one and last of the adopted children was Maria Theresa, and I could find her in New York City. I went to see her perform; she was dancing to Franz Liszt's "Les Funerailles," wearing a heavy white cape draped on her body in the Grecian style, she was mourning a dying soul, of which appeared that she was grieving the dying souls of all humanity. I had never been moved to tears by any dancer before, and I truthfully became confused and thought to myself, *I thought Isadora Duncan was dead*! She truly carried her spirit so powerfully, that it was overwhelming, and completely changed the course of my life. It seemed, that all of her gestures originated from a deep inner, heartfelt center and radiated outward, expressing profound feelings of humanity, wisdom, grace, naturalness, and nobility, thereby elevating the human drama of life to a higher, all encompassing, strong, and beautiful level of expression, a truly divine art. The dance, she stated, was a different way of living a more harmonious, gentle existence, and one could express gestures that all of humanity could relate to. As a person, she was loving, gentle yet strong, generous, kind, good natured, and everything a noble person could be. Following the Performance, I had the opportunity to meet her, and we instantly had a deeply felt spiritual connection, a knowing that this was a kindred soul. What was also so remarkable about her was that she was the same person offstage as she was on. Her main message throughout our friendship was that the dance should be natural, that Isadora detested imitators and mechanical movements. Theresa thus became a sister, a mother, a best friend, and a master Teacher. As we lived in basically the same area in New York City, we met regularly for many years, going practically every weekend to the Metropolitan Museum of Art and conversing for hours on her life with Isadora, her husband Stephan Bourgeois and her two sons, Rano and Feodor, and Violet, Rano's wife, whom were always there for her. Rano, whom she named after the Egyptian Sun God, radiated with a brilliant light, like the sun at all times. He carried the same loving and generous personality of his mother! During the week we would go to the YWCA and practice for three hours a session on the dances until the "Funeral March" and "Presto, Sonata in B minor Op. 35" by Chopin, Franz Liszt's "Les Funérailles" and Beethoven's Seventh Symphony in A major, Op. 92, which she referred to as "your dance; or the light soul leading the darker shades of the soul towards the light." She also told me that the cape was my forte', and that I understood the art of the dance better than anyone she knew. I had already lived in Europe and had studied the great masters in Florence and Paris, so I had these visual images already in my mind's eye, therefore the dance came naturally to me. She encouraged me to also create, or recreate, movements that were my own; in other words, she brought out your own unique individuality and nurtured your creative spirit. She was content and still with reverence during the creative act. It was truly a wonderful experience working with her. She didn't use too many words; she was able to transmit her ideas instantaneously, with a few gestures, some explanation, and the music; and I automatically responded, like magic, and understood what she was transmitting. She said she used Isadora's Universal Principles of Movement because they were in harmony with nature, and revealed the truth in motion, and at the same time created hundreds of dances of her own, which I believe she was the only one out of the six adopted daughters to do so. Of course she was also blessed with a wonderful, supportive, and talented husband who played the piano magnificently while she danced. Stephan Bourgeois had one of the most important art galleries in New York City, and exhibited the works of Marcel Duchamp. He also lectured at the Metropolitan Museum of Art. She possessed this innate ability to create to the music after having grown up with the great genius Isadora. She also possessed this *flame-like*, powerful presence on the stage, and was able to make a strong impact on the audience as Isadora had. With a simple gesture, a raising of an arm that contained such an enormous emotional content, she was able to transmit the meaning of the gesture, with such a sustained strength and conviction to the audience, and they magnanimously responded. She said she understood the psyche of the great composers—like Franz Liszt, Tchaikovsky, Schubert, Wagner, and Beethoven, and from that point of departure, was able to interpret the music through their mind's eye, movements creating a visual tone picture. Yes, Theresa possessed her own creative genius!

With the aid of her wonderful husband Stephan, whom she loved deeply, they created together. He danced on the piano, as she envisioned the movements that became an architectural tone painting. What a wonderful love story. She built her dance upon the structure of a composition following with sure instinct, the great artists, painters, and musicians such as Michelangelo, Beethoven, Wagner, Botticelli, and Gluck!

Hearing Theresa describe the "Isadorian Dance " as she called it revealed to mind the great artists that knew, saw, and understood Isadora's Great Art. So it is that I was able to understand the Art from living and studying the great masters of Florence and Paris.

Sibelius was the last dance that she created and worked on until ninety years old. Full of light, great, beauty, harmony, and all that was good and pure, it was truly a transcendent experience, something hard to explain, for a new creation was born. She radiated like a beacon of Light that emanated from her Soul, pulsating and expanding outward in curvilinear light waves until her whole being, body and soul, surrendered to God.

Everyday coming to the museum reminds me of all our visits to the Metropolitan Museum, and I feel closer to the great artist and Divine woman. She was also physically beautiful—with a pre-Raphaelite type of beauty, and naturally vibrant, thick, lush red hair; with high exotic cheekbones; and sparkling electric almond-shaped blue eyes, a small frame, very feminine—a true divine being, closer to being a Priestess than a mortal!

She totally lived the art of the dance. Every atom and cell of her body had been impregnated by this extraordinary *divine art form in motion* that Isadora had originally discovered. Theresa transmitted Isadora's art from its depth, its source, and recreated in the same light as Isadora had! Isadora did not want people to imitate her dances—they were her own soul's creations. She was the sole *creator,* or author, and they could not be successfully imitated. Rather she devised a technique based on the laws of nature—the ebb and flow of the ocean, the swaying of trees, the motion of the winds, the flight of birds—movements to which all human creatures could relate because they were movements in harmony with nature and the whole Universe. What better Music could she have chosen than the great classical musicians Beethoven, Schubert, Bach, Liszt, and Brahms, for they also penetrated universal laws of sound in order to create music that provoked emotion and passion such as joy, sorrow, death, birth, and redemption. These musicians portrayed great human drama in their music! That is Isadora's great genius: She understood the psyche of the musician, as she herself was a great artist and genius, and she created dances with that idea in mind. Visually she impregnated her mind's eye with great works of art and sculpture and returned to the Greeks, where classical beauty, harmony, and symmetry prevailed. The form of the body was elevated to a work of art by adorning it with flowing tunics, which allowed the greatest of freedom in movement. All of the artists who wrote about her understood what she represented, such as Rodin, Bourdelle, de Sogenzac, Eleanor Duse, Arnold Genthe, Edward Steichen, Gordon Craig, Louis Sue, Walkowitz, and others. It was these great artists who wrote about Isadora, and who most understood her, as did Maria Theresa, who was devoted to preserving the purity and truth in the art of Isadora's dance. That is the reason why she called it "my dance" (quote by Therese)—it was too all-encompassing for anyone to copy, so she stopped people from imitating it—because she thought it harmed her. After all, Theresa also possessed this extraordinary ability to create dances spontaneously to the music, creating forms that were reminiscent of great works of art and sculpting, that the great artists had created, but also in harmony emotionally with her bodily and facial expressions; understanding the music or piece of music heard, whether it be Schubert's "Raindrop Prelude," Sibelius, or Tchaikowsky's revolutionary piece.

Theresa taught in the same manner as Isadora. She discovered a variety of diverse themes: the first movement of fear, followed by reactions naturally originating from an initial emotion, that of sadness, that manifested into a dance of lamentation, or of love, that evolved into the softness of the petal of a flower. And that is how I learned the "Funeral March" of Chopin, the Franz Liszt -Les Funerailles, the Beethoven Seventh Symphony, and the Debussy-l'Apres-Midi-

d'un Faun, which Theresa had performed at the Theatre des Champs-Elysees in the 1930s. The initial or first movement triggered a sequence of movements, slowly mounting, reaching a crescendo, and returning, until the next movement was reborn; completing a circular form, which poured from the soul like water, and radiated like perfume to a level of ecstasy. It was finding your soul within!

Theresa was the only one of the six adopted daughters who did create so many of her own dances, and had the innate creative ability, and dedicated her whole life to keeping this great art form alive! She said to me, "Even if you're the only star in the sky, keep dancing, keep it alive, don't get lost!"

A session with Theresa would consist of a brief warm-up, not in the traditional sense. She always said, "Don't spend too much time on the exercises. Get right into the dances." She was like a beacon of light, arms raised high towards the Heavens, as if her whole being surrendered to a flood of Light from above, and was transformed into pure lightness and grace! We would start on Liszt's "Les Funerailles"; she would drape the cape on her body first, and then we would listen together with the same ear and soul to the music. She would explain a little of the Life of the Composer, and then the emotional and psychological motive of the piece, in very few words, so you would feel the same great passion as the Musician felt when he composed the music. Then we would proceed, with the first section portraying a mourning woman, weeping the death of her beloved at his funeral. She used her hands covering her face, head down; slowly lifting her head, back and forward again, in harmony with the musical phrase. Then as the music augmented in intensity, her arms extended to the front; her head thrown back, and hands clawing in a grieving, intense emotion. In the second phase, the upper torso and arms reached, down to the earth, and prayed up to the heavens in agony, until the crescendo reached a peak, and then was released, beginning a new musical phrase usually, slower and less intense. As I began to move, these gestures truly come out of an awakening or stirring, emanating from my own soul, and that's why they look like they were my own individual creations, but inspired and transmitted by Theresa, the master, but felt and expressed from my own *truth* in *motion*. The movements came like magic, as if I was carried along by the *wave of the music*, at one with the music in gesture, and this is how Isadora taught Theresa and how Theresa taught me; not simply learning choreography, but truly participating in a creative birth, portrayed in dance form to great music!

If I do nothing else in my whole life, it was indeed a great privilege in life to know Maria Theresa, one-of-a-kind extraordinary goddess-like light beings filled with inner and outer beauty, great depth of feeling, dignity, and humanity in her expression. Our many conversations over the span of ten years were a sure sign to me, as she had told me over and over again, that I must carry on this great art form, that I understood Isadora's art, and not to get lost wandering off.

Oh she brought tears to my eyes when I first saw Maria Theresa dance, and she still moved me twenty years later; that someone so extraordinary existed, and that I was blessed enough to know her well for nearly ten years both as a friend, a teacher, in a truly spiritual sense. I felt as if I was in the presence of a divine, and radiantly beautiful being, full of grace, harmony, naturalness, and gentleness of gesture and movement. She taught me how to create dances in the truly creative spirit to the music. The dances were her choreography with certain passages of my own—which she greatly supported, with respect and reverence, when I responded to the movement, spontaneously creating my own interpretation, but in harmony with the art forms of the dance. Thus I come to understand on a deep plane what Isadora had originally invented; movements originating from the solar plexus or radiating from the heart center, outward, expressing truth, humanity, feeling, and naturalness, in harmony with music! Then it's a life worth living—for beauty, art, expression, the soul's yearning toward wholeness, completeness, balance, harmony, love, and light! It is the true Apotheosis of the Dance, and this, Isadora as no other dancer had revealed, and after her Maria Theresa, as told by all those who saw her dance. If I can speak of only a minute revelation of this great art form, then I have passed on something monumental!

Music as well as nature (the ocean) form curvilinear spheres, radiate in circles; therefore Isadora's genius was that she was the first to realize that dances depicting human drama—loss, love, anger, courage, despair, revolt, surrender—all of these emotions expressed through gesture by the body, could be spontaneous and in harmony with classical music, because the composers created music with the same idea in mind. As Isadora stated, she created more with the idea of expression rather than technique in mind. Theresa understood this theory so well, and that is how she could create in the same light as Isadora—and she projected a great human magnetism both on stage and off, as Isadora had!

She always said, "Study the lives of the musicians, understand their psyche, and the psychology of the particular piece of music." Depending on which emotion the music evoked—fear, anger, joy, revolt—this initial feeling triggered a corresponding sequence of movements that flowed of its own volition completing a musical phrase. Then you can start to create to the music using Isadora's principles of movement which were in harmony with nature, and all natural laws of motion and music. Chopin's Funeral March and Presto Sonate B minor Op. 35, was a dance defying death, resisting, fighting the inevitable, until we can no longer resist it and in the end we have no choice but to surrender to it! The Presto, however, symbolizes the resurrection of the soul after death. The eternal drama of the spirit over matter. The way she taught was with great humility, never domineering or egotistical, always with respect for you as an artist, in the midst of the creative act. She was extremely natural and would take the cape and say, for example, you can place it over your entire head, or just on your neck, revealing to me a few different ways of using the cape; and I would practice it until one or the other felt more natural, or felt more in harmony with the music. She was able to feel the music, with such profound emotion that she needed not speak nor analyze the sequence of movement in too fine a detail, because it was rather through osmosis and intuition that the movement was communicated to me. I responded both naturally and spontaneously, and she would simply nod her head with approval. We worked on that dance many times, going over each section until it was perfected! I must add that; she did not explain, she rather taught by inspiration! She danced or indicated by a gesture. She believed that art should be taught on the *wings* of genius. You could not learn it, you grasped it intuitively, spontaneously, like a *flash of lightning*! The spark within you must turn into the flame. It was an inner unfoldment that could not be forced artificially. If you had the "eye" to see and the spirit to grasp it, her dancing offered to each beholder a working dream of an aspiring, unsuspected self. It was in this light that Theresa danced to the great works of Liszt's "Les Funerailles," Chopin's "Funeral March," and Beethoven's Seventh Symphony, Debussy, Tchaikovsky's "Marche Slave"—intuitive and improvisatory to a high degree, yet always creative and passionate! The whole composition was based on the surge and mood inherent in the music and thus becomes a wondrous synthesis, where all the deeply visionary, dramatic, and musical gifts of the artist are expressed, shine and radiate! I myself stopped dancing for several years when my Father and Theresa passed away, and my health wasn't good—I went to live in France to restore my health. I was strongly led back to the dance to continue the legacy of Maria Theresa, and all she had passed on to me and that there was a reason that I was to have such a long and private relationship with her, and that she chose me to teach these great works with the cape that no one else knows.

Theresa seemed like a muse, timeless, eternal, representing all that is truthful, beautiful, and human through the dance!

"This is the miracle that after Isadora there should come one who can lift our spirits and by her beautiful dancing. Take us up into the heights of beauty."

She touches our souls to the quick and fills us with exultant joy. Her name is Maria Theresa.
—Toni Sides
Paris–New York, December 1937

PAMELA DE FINA

Maria Theresa, 1986, New York City
during one of our practices
Photo by Pamela De Fina

Working with Theresa was like creating a dance poem. One starts with a story, creates gestures that interpret the story put into motion, and with the aid of the music, a new dance is born. Starting slowly, passions mounting, building to a climax, and release to begin again. Theresa also said that Isadora's brother Augustin taught her a lot about acting!

There seems to be a general confusion in the mind of the public at large, whether or not there was a technique to Isadora's dances. My experience was that there is no doubt that there is a definite technique. Even Maria Theresa, who created many dances of her own clearly stated, that she used Isadora's universal laws of the balance of all natural phenomena—ocean waves, the forward and backward movements of expansion and contraction of the body in rhythm with the ever changing nuances of the music. The clear contrast between up and down, rising and falling, as the body yields itself, not passively but actively to the music. The gesture itself starts softly, takes on a shape or form; mounts and becomes stronger and more intense, than the previous one! Of course there was a definite bar, and precise choreography that Duncan passed on through her sister Elizabeth and the adopted daughters; but Isadora, as Theresa was, a genius and a great artist with a dynamic, magnanimous, and radiant personality. She was no teacher in the ordinary sense. Isadora taught by inspiring. She indicated by gesture the movements. And that is how I learned the dances from Theresa. She always said, "Don't do Isadora Duncan dances. She didn't want people to; she said those were the creations of her own soul," therefore Theresa created her own! Thus it was that most of the dances transmitted to me were directly from Theresa. Section by section, we worked on them until they were perfected. She used few words, but more creative, inventive ideas that I intuitively grasped instantaneously because we were on the same wavelength. There were certain passages in which she encouraged me to be spontaneous, to create, to invent myself to the felt experience, with the music, and thus new movements were born. She naturally brought out my own creativity or uniqueness, the transposition of musical thought into dance. It was the music that provoked a giving gesture of motion! Working with Theresa was a totally creative experience; for her innate ability to express her idea and passions in a musical sensibility, creating a complete artistic picture or drama! The way she began the piece was first to listen to the music and fully comprehend its psychic contents and that of the composer as well. She would discuss a little of the life and psychological state of the composer. Then she would start the music, beginning with the purple cape, as in Chopin Funeral March, draped on her body so that you could maneuver it in such a way that it became definitely an integral part of the dance. In this dance, the predominant theme is death, therefore, I had to deeply feel the loss of a loved one or, feel the loss of someone you love, or your own eventual doom. Then she would begin very naturally, walking first and dropping her head toward the earth and then back and upwards towards the heavens, then with the aid of the upper torso and arm until a whole segment or musical phrase was complete with gesture and movement expressed through the music—and actually grew in form, and in harmony with the music, like something magical, but totally natural. She was able to fuse all musical, artistic, and psychological elements together, and create a work of art, or total picture that evolved into a complete dance from beginning to end! And it was the same with each dance that she created. Liszt's "Les Funerailles" was a somewhat more difficult dance. She would start the same way, first with the drapery on the body like a Greek sculptural piece. And then she would start with head down, hands covering her face, as the gesture heard from within started growing; first by raising the head up and back, and then down again, then as the music and the dance became more intense her arms were outstretched with a passionate, emotional rage and sadness while mourning the death of the poet Plutarch. At the third musical sequence her entire body was enveloped with remorse! Her basic gestures were natural; up and down and backward and forward. She would begin a gesture with emotion; softly, gently, subtly, utter a few words sometimes, but mostly with gestures. In certain passages there was *space* to be creative, and I made motions with the cape to the music as if a *spirit* had descended upon me and enraptured my entire being. They complemented the piece and Theresa was happy with what I had created. So I videotaped them and along with her, we went to the Library of the Performing Arts to present the video before she died. The video is called "Spiral of Life."

It was uncanny that my father should get ill at the same time Theresa did. They both were taken to the hospital and died within one year. I can still remember the last visit to the Metropolitan Museum. I fetched her at the hospital and took her in a wheelchair, and she sat in front of one of the great masterpieces and became fixated on it. Her soul was elevated, dear soul that she was, and then she fell asleep! I can still see her face all lit up, electric, magnetic, beautiful—she's what gives me life these days. After she and my father died, my life has been a struggle. Yes, I returned to Theresa and the dance with more emotional maturity, with a deeper understanding of everything that Theresa and Isadora's philosophy of life and beauty in movement represented!

The last piece we were working on was Debussy -Apres-Midi d'Un Faune, as she called it and said she performed that in Paris at the Theatre des Champs-Elysees. It began: A nymph sleeping on a bench in the woods, begins slowly raising her head, as she hears the music, and then goes back to sleep, and then begins rising first just with the torso, the arms begin swaying like branches of a tree, and playfully, the nymph sees a fawn, and starts flirting with him.

Then she impishly jumps off the bench to play with the fawn, first darting to one side, then to the other. Theresa was dancing her last piece before she died, which was "Sibelius." She looked and appeared like a beacon of light radiating *spirals* of energy to the *heavens*: She reached upward and the heavens responded. They showered her with the grace and *beauty* from above that only those truly great human beings are endowed with. I receive so much enlightenment from this most generous loving soul! We spent long hours, particularly in the Greek Art department at the Metropolitan Museum, where she said Isadora had the Athena statue and sculpture of dancing children in their school at Darmstadt, Germany. I felt that I was conversing with a living icon, a classical sculpture of Aphrodite, that had come to Life! By her very presence and gentle manner of communicating, she lifted you up and out of this banal dimension of reality, with all its pettiness and jealousies, onto a transcendent sphere, where only *spiritual beings* live. How fortunate was I to have all this private time with Theresa, just she and I! Just to think of Theresa always brings sadness to the inner depths of my soul. I know I must persevere and continue this art form which symbolizes and expresses life, breath, wholeness, and beauty of the soul; as Rodin, and Michelangelo whose sculptures depicted harmony in natural form, based on curvilinear lines, as the ocean waves, the pulsation of light rays in the air, and the vibration of sound !

In the beginning was Song,
Dance is born of Song as love is born of the heart. A. Bourdelle

Maria Theresa's Early Years

Maria Theresa, originally named Theresa Kruger, was chosen by Isadora Duncan for her "new school of the future," founded in Grunewald, Germany, in 1905. Theresa, who was then nine years old, was born near Dresden, of a Polish mother and a German father. She vividly recalled, even in her eighties, the sequence of events which precipitated her fate. Isadora arrived in Berlin, Germany in January 1905 for performances, and to find students for her new School in Berlin. She came to watch our simple, child-like- Christmas pageant, that I and my sisters were dancing in. While I was dancing, I noticed a divinely serene woman sitting in the loge, close to the stage, dressed in a white Grecian tunic, with a scarf wrapped around her body, and up over her head, she appeared like a White Angel. She was smiling so sweetly at me, that I forgot my dance, while our gazes locked. The next day, she came to my house. When the doorbell rang, I answered the door and there stood the same White Angel in her Greecian tunic and scarf. Not since the days of Christ had anyone dressed like she, especially in the winter with snow on the ground. As she entered my house, she told me that she wanted to take me away to her School in Berlin. She invited my Mother, my sisters and myself to her performance the next day. The huge audience was spellbound, at her performance. My Mother asked me if I wanted to learn to dance like that, seeing the beauty of it. "I said softly, Yes. She said, then, you will have to leave me. Two days later I went to the Hotel where Isadora Duncan was staying, along with a few other children she had chosen in a similar fashion. Gordon Craig answered the door and said, Isadora, your children are here. As Theresa described this event, her face lit up, radiating with joy. "Isadora came along at the right psychological moment," she said. A Renaissance was taking place in the Arts: a time of innovation, a Greek revival, a return to classical antiquity, music, and art. Isadora's School of the Future was an experiment in a new way of life, offering larger expression. The school's popularity grew rapidly throughout Germany, which was then the center of European culture. Theresa said that she performed for all the royalty of Germany and that "The King of Bavaria sent his carriage to bring me to his medieval castle where I taught dance to his children." She said she also danced for King Edward VII, the Queens of Naples, and of Greece. Maria Theresa vividly remembered meeting Anna Pavlova during their first voyage to St. Petersburg, Russia, in 1908. "She always brought us lots of chocolate," she said of Anna. She also spoke of Anna's remarkable grace, lightness, and the fluidity of her arms in her performance of the "Dying Swan."

Isadora Duncan reported in her book, My Life, "While at the Parthenon in 1920, Edward Steichen, who was one of our party, took many lovely pictures on the Acropolis, in the Theatre of Dionysius, which faintly foreshadowed the splendid vision I longed to create in Greece." Isadora, Theresa, and her adopted sisters accidently met Edward Steichen in Athens, who borrowed a Kodak camera from a hotel waiter, immortalizing the dancers and some of their most exquisite photographs, of which "Wind Fire," one of the most famous, is published in this book and was first published in "A Life of Photography" (New York: Doubleday, 1963). They were taken in the afternoon while the sun was setting, projecting golden rays of light in the background with a magnificent view of the ocean. Steichen wrote that Theresa was "the most talented of Isadora's protegees." He also stated: "...unlike Isadora, she had no feelings of conflict. She was a living reincarnation of a Greek nymph." He was ingenious for capturing the projection of her soul in motion! Recalling her dancing in Greece in 1920, she remarked: "I stand transfixed in contemplation in the precinct of the temple...I raise my arms to the sky...the sun melts in a splendor of burnt gold. The evening breeze sighs among the columns, against the flaming sky...I dance the glory of the heavens and of the human spirit, and my Dance becomes a prayer, an invocation and a benediction...so my dancing reveals the intimation of yet a greater Spirit that moves me to dance...It demands a great soul to dance great music and project its inherently magnanimous spirit...And that is the secret of my dancing; to feel deeply, to touch life, to be as the flame in the wind. All this imaginative expressive dancing was based on the music as I felt it, danced with my body aglow and tingling with life."

Maria Theresa was the first dancer to be invited as the guest of Eleanor Roosevelt to give a concert at the White House on May 2, 1933. Not only was she invited to perform; she was also privileged to be a houseguest of the Roosevelts for several days thence.

Maria Theresa often told me that the dance needs a *"new spirit."* She was the *new spirit*— the Art of the Isadorian dance *resurrected* through her! Isadora, who died at fifty, was tragically strangled by the same red silk scarf that had symbolized *life* for her as a woman and in her *art*. She was haunted by death until it finally snatched her suddenly!

Theresa represented the positive, *joy-filled*, exalted side of *Isadora*. No one after Isadora was capable of portraying Isadora's art with the depth of understanding and creative genius as Maria Theresa. She was the personification of all the wisdom of the ancient sages—the great ones of mankind expressed through the art of the dance. She was the *Flame in the Wind*, the living manifestation of beauty and serenity and grace exalted to a virtually *Divine Order*, speaking her own language, yet always gently moving in rhythm to the *sound* of *higher order* expressing love, humanity, joy, and a greater generosity inspiring all who were in her presence! She was the *way* and the *light*! And her name is:

MARIA THERESA.

"Wind Fire" Theresa Duncan, Athens, Greece, 1921
Photo taken by Edward Steichen
© 2021 The Estate of Edward Steichen / Artists Rights Society (ARS), New York.
Courtesy George Eastman House

Maria Theresa, Munich 1921
With permission to publish without reservation
from Rano Bourgeois, son of Maria Theresa.

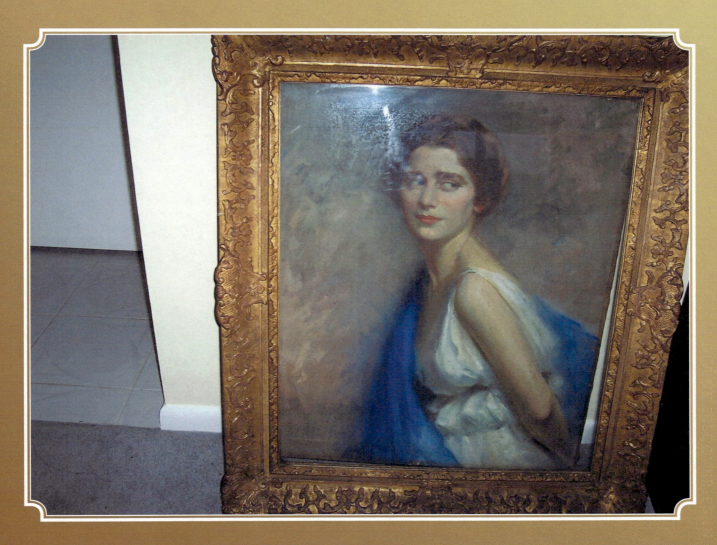

Pastel Painting of Maria Theresa Duncan, artist unknown, given by Rano Bourgeois, Theresa's son, to Pamela De Fina who took this photo.

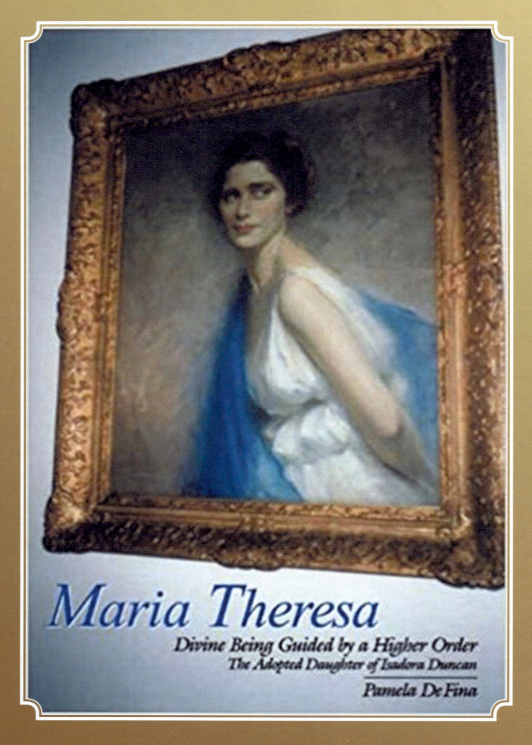

Maria Theresa
Divine Being Guided by a Higher Order
The Adopted Daughter of Isadora Duncan

Pamela De Fina

Painting of Maria Theresa, that I was given by her son. I decided to write this book right after the death of Maria Theresa in 1987, as the experience with her was still very much alive and deeply profound. I was living in NYC on E. 74th st, and she on E. 83rd st right near the Metropolitan Museum where we frequented on the weekends, after practicing at the Y studio 3 times a week. 3 hours at a time. It was a deeply mystical and highly creative experience, as she became a master teacher, best friend., and soul mate. I was chosen by her for her Heritage group first appearing at the United Nations, as her Protogee. In 1979.

"Maria Theresa and the Heliconiades"
Permission to publish without reservation by Rano Bourgeois,
son of Maria Theresa

Theresa was celebrated as the greatest musical dramatic soloist of her day. Theresa stated : " Isadoras art cannot be explained. This was not a system of steps,but a deep understanding of the workings of the Universe, and a profound wisdom to see with an inner vision, the progression of musical figures in the development of a composition, in harmony with the music.

Edward Steichen, Marie Therese, Hym to the Sun. 1921, Athens, Greece. In Life of Photography, ©
2021 The Estate of Edward Steichen / Artists Rights Society (ARS), New York, Steichen was able
to borrow a Kodak camera, and slowly Isadora Duncan warmed to the idea of being photographed.
However Steichens photographs of Maria Theresa at the Parthenon and on the Acropolis are the
more memorable, He stated,"Theresa who was,I felt the most talented of them. Unlike Isadora,
she had no feelings of conflict. She was a living reincarnation of a Greecian Nymph".

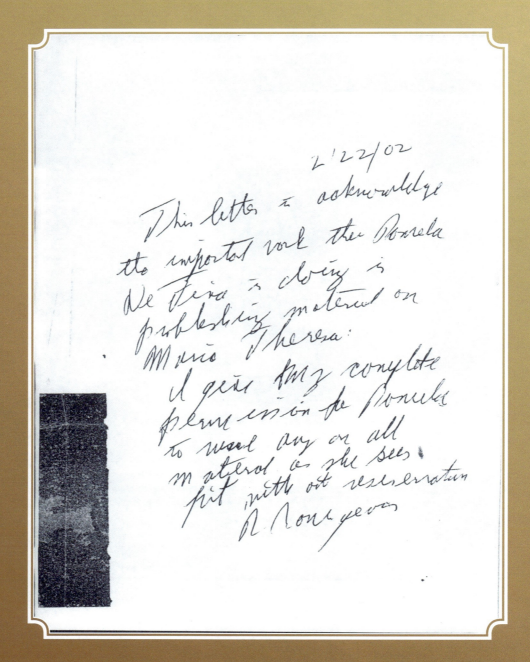

2/22/02

This letter to acknowledge the important work that Pamela De Fina is doing publishing material on Maria Theresa:

I give my complete permission to Pamela to used any or all material as she sees fit with out reservation

R. Bourgeois

This Letter given to me by Rano Bourgeois, son of Maria Theresa: stating: " This letter is to acknowledge the important work that Pamela De Fina is doing publishing material on Maria Theresa, I give my complete permission to Pamela, to use any or all material as she sees fit without reservation" signed R. Bourgeois..

Pamela de Fina

STEICHEN carousel 236 West 26th Street, New York, New York 1000]

Permission Agreement for use of photograph(s) by Edward Steichen controlled, owned or in possession of Joanna T. Steichen.

(1) *White Fire*
(2) *HT in Acropolis*
(3) *HT, Isadora Anna on acropolis*
(4) *Isadora*
(5) *HT–G–W.F.*
(6) *Isadora on acropolis*

Date: *13 September, 1999*

1. Edward Steichen photograph(s) to be reproduced:

2. Use of photograph(s): The photograph(s) described in Clause 1 shall be reproduced on a non-exclusive basis, for one-time only, in one publication, for one edition, in the following publication:

TITLE: *The Pamela de Fina*
Maria Serrata; Divine Being...
AUTHOR:

PUBLISHER/PUB. DATE: *Dorrance Press, Philadelphia 2001*

3. Territorial Grant: The photograph(s) described in Clause 1 shall be circulated for sale in the publication described in Clause 2 only in the following parts of the world:

4. Credit Line: Wherever the photograph(s) described in Clause 1 appears, the following credit line shall appear in a suitable position.

REPRINTED WITH PERMISSION OF JOANNA T. STEICHEN

5. Payment: The following sum shall be paid upon acceptance by you on the terms of this Agreement for the non-exclusive, one-time only usage described above:

$ _____ photograph for North American Rights Only.

$ *100 prs* photograph for World Rights/*All Languages, all editions*

$ _____ photograph for the following territories/languages.

6. Warranty and Guarantee: Joanna T. Steichen warrants & guarantees that she may grant this permission.

7. Complimentary copies: You agree to send two complimentary copies of the publication in which the work appears to Carousel Research at the above address

8. Confirmation: This Agreement is to be signed and returned to Carousel Research, Inc. with your payment (made out to Carousel Research, Inc.) of $ *600* Permission will be granted only when Carousel Research, Inc. returns a signed copy for your files.

9. Prints: All prints are to be returned to **STEICHEN/carousel** after use.

AGREED TO: _____

Signature _____ Date _____ Carousel Research, Inc.
on behalf of Joanna T. Steichen

Please note photos can be requested on George
Eastman House Mu curator David Hockin

Tel. 212–255–8100 Fax 212–255–8107 Telex 6973124 LPW CM

fax 716–271–3970
Allen Clark

Permission by Joanna Steichen for my book. In 1999.

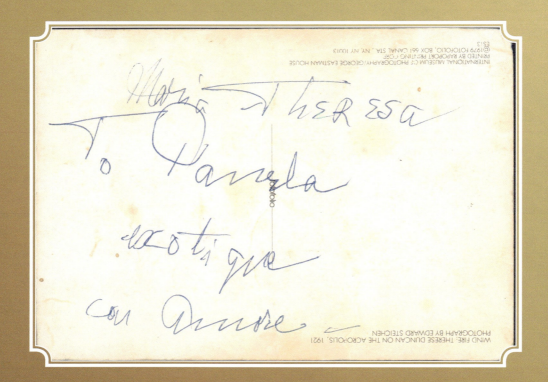

Maria Theresa signature-"To Pamela exotique Con Amore, Maria Theresa.

Maria Theresa and Stephan Bourgeois- Husband- unknown photographer

The "Classical Dance"

A great deal has been written about the dance-form, which Isadora Duncan rediscovered and I have been pursuing in the last decades with equal fascination.

For all those, who actually have been able to penetrate the mysteries of the "Classical Dance", it is easy to see, that it is not a system of steps, but rather the spontaneous perception of Life's perennial values, compounded Tragedy and Joy, to use Nietzsche's words, underlying always life's experience and necessary to the very creation of any real art.

Since this attitude is also the secret of great composers, their work serves ideally as the essential life-tissue of the Dance, because the concordance of music is the essential current which carries the course of the dance to new vistas.

In the absence of any mechanical theory, the public is therefore expected to abandon itself to the passing moment, advancing freely into an invisible world, presently becoming visible through Perennial Classicism... as old as the Western World's root in ancient Greece and as young as the coming future.

Maria Theresa
January 1954.

"You, Theresa, have the imprint of Dionysos' kiss on your brow."

—Isadora Duncan

"Tu hai la fiamma sacra nel cuore."

—Eleanor Duse

"Again and again, last evening, it seemed to me, that I was watching Isadora herself, as I saw her dance some forty years ago. The physical resemblance to my memory of her was breathtaking; the intensity of effect was identical! But I always realized that it was you, not she, that was dancing...that you made her concept your own, have developed it, have carried it forward into provinces, where she did not and could not venture..."

—Lloyd Morris, MARCH 29, 1949

"This is the miracle! That after Isadora there should come one who can lift our spirits and by her beautiful dancing take us up into the heights of beauty...She touches our souls to the quick and fills us with exultant joy...her name is MARIA-THERESA."

—Fredo Toni Sides, DECEMBER 1952

"...When Maria Theresa dances, we are moved beyond time and space: her interpretations are incomparable... every dance is four dimensional: it is a work of art; it is drama; it is poetry; it is musical and visionary; and it is supremely and triumphantly human."

—George Metzger, Cuban Composer, MARCH 1953

"...The dances of Maria-Theresa are all idyll...invocation...tragic grandeur and exaltation... mythical rapture and passion...She wrought before us with astounding rhythmic phrase and expression and movement, a vision of beauty and poetry. Every gesture becomes an illumination..."

—Shaemas O'Sheal, NOVEMBER 1951

"...She has the greatness of spirit and generosity of soul of the true artist...her dances are poems ...She danced the mystery of the human heart...her dancing is all joy...intensely dramatic and always beautiful. It is alive with the glory of the spirit..."

—Mrs. Sidney Lanier, FEBRUARY 1952

"...It is a miraculous union, this dancing and the music. Whatever the music, she caught the power and the vision and built upon it with real inspiration..."

—Desire Defaw

"...Here is dance in its loveliest guise...a radiant vision...exquisite dancing...extraordinary power and concentration...fiery temprament...all grace...and profoundly moving...She is music incarnate..."

—Mrs. Robert Flaherty

"...A beautiful figure and a limpid spirit...The dancing of Maria-Theresa is pure illumination...Seeing her dance is to know that we have been in the company of great spirits...So great and beautiful and true!..."

—Vladimir Sokoloff, FEBRUARY 1951

"…Hers is the ideal and a fiery heart …the vision and the greatness of soul…a beautiful dancer and a great artist…her dances are poems … she dances the mystery of the human soul…Maria-Theresa is an artist of tremendous power, integrity and passionate conviction…She is unique…"

—*Louis Jouvet, April 1951*

"…A deeply moving experience…a lovely dancer…an incandescent mind…She takes us to the heights of joy and tragic grandeur…"

—*Louis K. Anspacher*

"Maria-Theresa holds us enthralled…utterly enchanting…Her performance is a magic of imagining…an improvisation strangely blended of rhapsody and tragedy, joy, breauty and profundity…"

The Relationship Between Music and Dance

Theory

In one of Theresa's programs it states that Maria Theresa gave a dance recital and lecture at Clark University, Worcester, making a new experience of explaining her dances. By outlining the context of the *music*, the *dramatic idea* of the *composer* was manifested with absolute clarity to the spectator. Isadora Duncan stated: "Her interpretation combines with an elemental spontaneity makes music actually *visible* to the eye like a *drama"* This *method* has proven to be of the greatest educational value. Her success in creating new compositions and new forms and ideas has given Maria Theresa the distinguished position of the most dramatic solo dancer of our time.

Likewise Isadora stated: "Plunge your soul in divine unconscious, giving deep within it, until it gives to your soul, its secret. That is how I have always tried to express *music*—my *soul* should become one with it, and the *dance* born from that *embrace. Music* has been in all my life the great inspiration, and will be perhaps someday the consolation, for I have gone through such terrible years. No one has understood since I lost Deirdre and Patrick how pain has caused me at times to live in almost a delirium. In fact my poor brain has more after been crazed than anyone can know. When you think of these years, think of the *Funeral Marche* of Schubert, the *Ave Marie*, the Redemption, and forget the times when my poor distracted soul trying to escape from suffering may well have given you all the appearance of madness. I have reached such high peaks flooded with light, but my soul has not strength to live there—and no one has realized the horrible torture from which I have tried to escape. Some day if you understood sorrow, you will understand all I have lived through and then you will only think of the light towards which I have pointed and you will know the *real Isadora* is there. In the meantime, work and create Beauty and Harmony. The poor world has need of it and with your six spirits going with one will you can create Beauty and Inspiration for a new life." — (*The Real Isadora*, p. 244.) Letter to six grown-up pupils dancing together as a group accompanied by the concert pianist George Copeland.

In *Isadora Duncan and the Basic Dance*, it states that the most important of all her approaches, other than stimulation by the other arts, was listen*ing to the music with her soul in order to stir the emotions.* She has told us nothing at all about her mode of procedure in these experiments; we find her deliberately invoking specific emotional states without music, and the only possible means within herself was memory. In order to discover a first movement of fear from which a sequence of related and developing movements should proceed in natural order, a state resembling fear itself must be recreated to stimulate the impulses of movement. This could only be done by recalling previous experiences of fear and allowing these memories to freely induce their own bodily and emotional states. "She did not carry the method itself through to its final development, and missed accordingly the basic technical process of her art," stated the author. However, her colleague Konstantin Stanislavsky carried the method through in another art form: the theater.

It was Maria Theresa, after Isadora, who created in the same light as Isadora, using the same approach. The *method* which she employed to stimulate the soul prior to movement was to *explain, using few chosen words*, the *psyche of the composer*, and what event in his life inspired him to write the music.

Music, as well as nature (the ocean, wind, clouds), forms curvilinear spheres radiating circles of magnetic light waves through the universe. Isadora Duncan was a forerunner, genius, and visionary to first recognize that dances depicting human drama, and expressing collective emotions through gestures could be spontaneous and in harmony with classical music, because the composers created musical pieces with the same philosophy in mind. Maria Theresa understood this principle deeply and entirely, body, mind, and soul! That is how she could create so many dances of her own, however resembling Isadora so strongly that I thought she was *Isadora*! She possessed a great human magnetism both on stage and off (like Isadora), but she was entirely herself; unique, whole, distinct; an individual in harmony with the universe at large!

In *Ma Vie*, Isadora stated: "It is an error to call me a dancer; I am rather a magnetic pole concentrated, that *translates the emotions of the music*! From my *soul emanate rayons of fire that unite with the orchestra vibrating and trembling at the same time!*" She also stated as early as 1904 (October 28 through November 4), while performing in St. Petersburg, Russia, for the Society for the Prevention of Cruelty to Children: *"I illustrate in my dances the thoughts of the composers,"* which is exactly what Maria Theresa transmitted in her teachings!

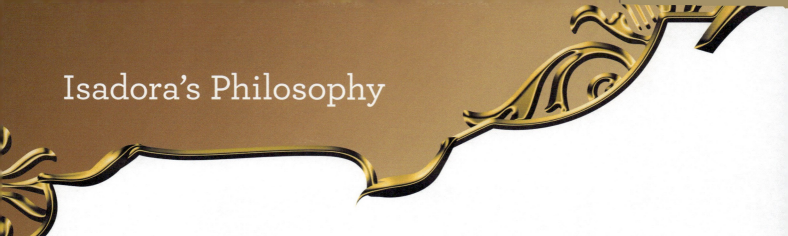

Isadora's Philosophy

"All movements on earth follow the great curvilinear lines. Sound travels in curves, radiates in circles, movements of water, wind, trees, plants all progress in curves. The flight of birds, and all animals, the movement of the clouds in the wind all follow circular lines. The base on which to develop human movement then is curvilinear as a point of departure. Movements must follow the rhythm of the ocean waves that rise, penetrate, and continue, that follow a cadence without end."

Ernst Haeckel, who wrote the Meaning of the Universe, stated that "my dance depicted all the universal truths in nature, and he said it was an expression of Monisme originating from a unique source and evolving into a unique sense."

Isadora's philosophy for the dance was founded on the principles of beauty and harmony of movement. She stated that the body must be forgotten; it's only an instrument whereby through movements it expresses the sentiments and thoughts of one's own soul. "In my school I found it possible to raise young girls in an atmosphere of beauty by placing before their eyes the ideal form to emulate continually by a perpetual practice of beautiful movement." She placed classical statutes of the ideal female form, Greek and Roman, to contemplate upon, incomparable grace, supple harmony, and beauty of their movements. "Imagine a dancer after long study and prayers, inspiration arrives to such a degree that her body transforms into a luminous manifestation of her soul while listening is penetrated by waves of divine music—the body is moved by the will of the music, this dance will be a message from another world."

Isadora Duncan at the Portals of Acropolis. Photo by Edward Steichen.1921. © 2021 The Estate of Edward Steichen / Artists Rights Society (ARS), New York, Courtesy of George Eastman House. Copy of original. " I often dance at the theatre of Dionysus, I stand in the center of the circle in the theatre while the gestures of my arms trace the lines of the architecture in front of me. I sense there how all elements fuse together harmoniously. The collaboration between tragic art and architecture are intimate. At the time of Sophocles: dance, poetry, music drama and architecture formed a harmonious whole union. I .Translated from an original text in French by p. de Fina.

"Isadora and Pupils" at the Parthenon, Caryatid Porch, Acropolis. Isadora, center, Maria Therese right, Anna, left. Photo by Edward Steichen,1921, © 2021 The Estate of Edward Steichen / Artists Rights Society (ARS), New York, Courtesy of George Eastman House. Copy of original. Theresas stongest wish was that she could remain in Greece, and teach at the school that Isadora had promised to establish there. However her dreams were shattered when Isadora, changed her plans suddenly, and they returned to Europe. Theresa often spoke of this journey to Athens with Isadora and the Isadorables with great passion,joy and regret. Isadora's study of the Greek art and culture became her most powerful source of inspiration in developing her Dance..

Maria Theresa from the collection of Rano Bourgeois

La Belle Epoch

Lecture

Isadora Duncan appeared in Paris, in 1900, at the dawn of a New Age, "La Belle Epoque." The period from 1900-14 witnessed many significant changes, like the birth of the camera, cinema, printing press, telephone, as well as new discoveries in the field of electricity made by the Curies. The new style within the arts was called Art Nouveau, which depicted a spiraling, curvilinear form symbolizing a deeper meaning of eternal, unending ebb and flow of universal energy. This S-shaped or spiraling symbolism was related to the applied arts—sculpting, jewelry, posters—and expressed the idea of motion. Human form was relegated to the fourth dimension (the flow of time), which is of a musical nature seen in the dance, where living man not only set in motion seen in the works of art, but also in the dance.

It was at the exciting Exposition Universelle 1900 that Isadora met Louis Fuller and Auguste Rodin. Isadora stated that, before her eyes, Louis Fuller transformed her garments into forms of lilies, flowers, butterflies, and magnificent multicolored orchards, which seemed to transmute into spirals! She was a magician of lights and colors, changing into fluid forms thousands of colored images! Louis Fuller was considered the apex of the Art Nouveau movement.

Isadora first visited the Rodin Pavilion, and from that time on she and Rodin became lifelong friends. Isadora said: *"Movement is the soul of all things."*

"I have always tried to express the inner feelings by the mobility of the muscles," said Rodin. Her idea of movement could be connected to the movement of the elemental forces in a grand design of cosmic unity shared by Rodin. "It can be said of Isadora that she has attained sculpture and emotion effortlessly. She has borrowed from nature that force which cannot be called talent but which is genius. Miss Duncan has unified life and the dance. She makes her dance sensitive to line and is as simple as the antiquity synonymous with beauty.'"

In 1905 Isadora left for St. Petersburg in Russia. She made a tremendous impact on the Ballet Russe, altering the style of the Ballet Russe for the first time. They began using the music of Chopin and Schuman, wearing Greek costumes, and taking off their slippers after her. Fokine's experiments with innovations in his choreography for Les Sylphides was reminiscent of Isadora, and with Nijinsky soon to explode onto the scene under the aegis of Diaghilev. She left for Moscow, where she performed an all-Chopin program, attended by Constantin Stanislavsky. He stated at about this period (1908 or 1909): "I never missed a single concert of hers. The necessity to see her often was dictated from within me by an artistic feeling that was closely related to her art. At that time I was in search of the very creative motor which the actor must learn to put in his soul before he comes on the stage."

From her book, *My Life*, she stated: "I spent long days and nights in the studio seeking that dance which might be the divine expression of the human spirit through the medium of the body's movement. For hours I would stand quite still, my two hands folded between my breasts, covering the solar plexus—but I was seeking and finally discovered the central spring of all movement, the crater of motor power, the unity from which all diversities of movements are born, the mirror of vision for the creation of the dance—it was from this discovery that was born the theory on which I founded my school."

Konstantin Stanislavsky was quoted at about this period (1908 or 1909): "I came to know the two great geniuses of this time who made a very strong impression on me—Isadora Duncan and Gordon Craig. The necessity to see her often was dictated from within me by an artistic feeling that was closely related to her art. Later, when I became acquainted with her methods as well as with the ideas of her great friend Craig, I came to know that in different corners of the world, due to conditions unknown to us, various people in various spheres sought in art for the same naturally born creature principles. At that time, I was in search of that very creative motor, which the actor must learn to put in his soul before he comes out on the stage. I watched her during performances and her rehearsals when her developing emotion would first change the expression on her face, and with shining eyes she would pass to the display of what was born in her soul. In remembering all our discussions of art and comparing what she did to what I was doing, it became clear to me that we were looking for one and the same thing in different branches of art." It was during this brilliant Parisian Period of the dancers' careers, with its apex, that the great sculptor Bourdelle began to make numerous sketches of Isadora. He stated: "To me it seemed that there, through her, was animated an ineffable frieze wherein Divine Frescoes slowly became human realities." Later at a soiree', he saw Isadora again dance with the phenomenal star of the Ballet Russe, Nijinsky. Thus it is that the Theatre des Champs-Elysees, one of the most beautiful in the world, is a great monument to Isadora. Later in 1913, Bourdelles again wrote: "When the great Isadora Duncan danced before me, fifty years of my life looking at all the great human masterpieces became suddenly animated in these planes, ordained from within by the spirit's aspiration." Speaking to some of his students long after the famous theater was built and decorated, Bourdelle said: "All my muses in the theatre are movements seized during Isadora's flight, she was my principal source." The murals by Maurice Denis above the stage, framing the ceiling, arc exquisite scenes of Maria Theresa and the adopted daughters of Isadora dancing amidst nature, depicting the three muses: Dance, Music, and Poetry. They are the most beautiful examples of Art Nouveau painting.

1913 Conference de Trocadero

On March 1913, Isadora Duncan, along with Auguste Rodin, Eugene Carriere, and Josephin Paladin, presented a series of conferences on the dance. The conference that she presented was titled, "Ce que doit etre la danse" ("The right place for the dance is the tragic chorus!). Dance separated from music, chanting, and other arts becomes decadence. At the time of Sophocles, dance, poetry, music, drama, as well as architecture formed a harmonious whole union; the different facets expressing the same emotion or sentiment, whether be it wisdom, reason, joy, prayer, sadness, or resignation. The collaboration between tragic art and architecture is intimate, nearly a fusion creating an image of the ideal man. The chorus is the center of the drama like the heart is the center of the human body. All elements converge to the chorus, and like rayons of pulsating light project outward. "At Athens, very early in the morning, I often dance at the Theatre of Dionysos. I sense there how all elements fuse together harmoniously. I stand in the center of the circle in the theatre, while the gestures of my arms trace the lines that follow those in front of me. The great musical geniuses understood rhythm. I dance the rhythm of the Bach, Gluck, Beethoven, Chopin, Schubert, and Wagner, because they soley understood and followed the rhythm of the human body. *The dance united with music and poetry becomes the tragic chorus.* That is the unique and sole goal of the dance; only then will it become an Art! *Tragedy is the masterpiece of the human Soul*! To give dance the prestige of being *Sacred*, that which it once was it is necessary for it to be reborn and take its original place, thereby fulfilling its true mission! Centuries before Eschyles, the Greek people danced. They expressed their feelings, whether they be joy, or sadness, or war, and from these dances the chorus was born; which became the father of all tragedy. From this unanimous chorus, Thespis became the first actor. The actor is often the poet in person, dialoguing with the chorus; revealing the events that are the subject of the poem. *The chorus then dances and sings and remains the Soul, or center of all the tragedy* which expresses the eternal ideals that govern Man, while the actors narrate the episodes and express the particular sentiment which becomes the Drama! Sophocles and Euripedes increased the number of actors; thereby reducing the chorus: Tragedy was born from the chorus. Tragedy died with death of the chorus! The theatre was then divided into two separate entities: the theatre of Music, and the speaking theatre. The most beautiful dream is to return to the idea of the theatre of Athens to rediscover the antique ideal; not to copy, nor to imitate but to inspire and recreate within ones deeper self, ones own personal inspiration, and to move towards the future!"

Isadora Duncan has no other theory than her own genius and instinct for rhythm. What is rhythm? It is harmonious encounter of the human soul with the Universal Laws in accord with one voice emanating from the musical spheres!

—Josephin Paladin 1913

Isadora Duncan has discovered the movements that are most spacious, most generous, that express strength, force, health, and noble sentiments; that is to say the human form in motion, expressing truthful feelings; for humanity has a diversity of fantastic ideas—but only one way of suffering, and tragedy is the apothesis of Sadness! (1913 Conference Trocadero, "Ce que doit etre la dance").

The dances that Maria Theresa taught me where originally created by Isadora; however Theresa danced her own unique interpretation, keeping in harmony with the Universal Principals that Isadora had originally discovered. It is an interesting coincidence that Richard Wagner in his *Art Works of the Future* said that the Beethoven Seventh Symphony is the "Apothesis of the Dance," and that Miss Duncan should have danced the Symphony for the first time before Cosima Wagner; after having studied the composition for five years prior, Isadora's interpretation was the movement of the Universe concentrated in an individual, becoming what is termed the will. For example, the movement of the earth being the concentration of surrounding forces gives to the earth its individuality, its will. The dance should be the natural gravitation of this will in the individual, The human translation of the gravitation of the universe the dance. The Greeks were the greatest students of the laws of nature, wherein all is the expression of unending, ever increasing evolution, with no beginnings and no endings. *"For art which is not religious is not art, it is mere merchandise." The dance of the future will have to become again a high religious art as it was with Greeks.* The Danse Forest Press, 15 East 34 street, New York, New York, 1909 by (Isadora Duncan).

In 1909 she performed the Beethoven Seventh Symphony in the Criterion Theatre, and at the Metropolitan Opera House, New York

In 1909 she performed the Beethoven Seventh Symphony in the Criterion Theatre, and the Metropolitan Opera House, New York City. "As soon as he intensified the force of the crescendo, the life force raised in me in the form of a gesture. **At each musical phrase is translated into a musical movement my entire being vibrated in harmony with the music"** Isadora Duncan, *The Dance*, 1909. At the same performance, was Teddy Roosevelt who defended Isadora against tile unfair protests of certain *pasteurs*! His words were reported in all the papers. —*"Quel mal ces pasteurs peuvent-ils voir aux danses d'Isadora?"* It appeared to me that she was as innocent as an infant dancing in the garden under the morning sun gathering beautiful flowers of her dreams."

Bellevue 1913-1914

Mon Lohengrin (Paris Singer), *mon Chevalier du graal* had declared his love for me, and I was certainly in love and happy. Lohengrin had an apartment in Place des Vosges. I felt like I was alive again with a new and joyful manner that I had never known before. His love transported and elevated me in his white wings that ravished me in a golden cloud. I also seemed to know the best restaurants in Paris through him, where he was treated like a god. At Versailles in the park, Lohengrin held a *grande fete*. The banquet lasted until midnight and the gardens were illuminated with the sound of the Viennise orchestra and people danced until the morning.

Paris Singer (Lohengrin) told Isadora that he bought the Grand Hotel of Bellevue, where the gardens descended to the river and the rooms could lodge a thousand children. The next day we visited Bellevue together with the decorators and tapisseries under my direction. We transformed this rather banal hotel into a Temple of Dance for the Future. Fifty candidates were chosen to be the first students. The dance rooms had been previous dining rooms of the old hotel, adorned with my blue curtains. The *salle a manger* was arranged after the *modele* of the Chambrides Communes with the seats in gradated rows. The highest seats were reserved for the students who were oldest, Theresa, Irma, Anna, Lisel, *professeurs,* and the others for the children. In the midst of this *vie agitee* I found the courage to teach my students with *extraordinaire rapidite.* At the end of three months their progress was such that they aroused the admiration of all the artists that came to watch them. Saturday was the day of Artists, a public lesson in their honor was held in the morning 11:00 A.M. to 1:00 P.M., and afterwards, thanks to the generosity of Paris Singer, *un grand dejeuner* was served to the artists and students together. When it was good weather, the *dejeuner* was served in the garden to music, poetry, and dance. Rodin, whose villa was opposite at Meudon, came often to see us. He sat in the *salle de danse* with his sketchbook, drawing the young girls and children while they danced. One day he said to me, "If I had had such models when I was young whose movements are in accord with nature and harmony. I've had magnificent models, it's true, but none that understand the science of movement like your students do."

The day at Bellevue began with an explosion of joy. The voices of the children chanted all together as their little feet ran along corridors. I found them in the *salle de danse*, as they screamed in a chorus, "Bonjour, Isadora." How could I be sad in that atmosphere? Certainly sometimes I would, search for the little faces that had disappeared and I would run to my room and cry all alone; however I found the force to reprendre chaque jour my teaching and it was the charming grace of the children that encouraged me to live. Each week many artists came to Bellevue with their albums of designs as the school became known as a source of inspiration. Some hundred sketchbooks were filled with dancing figures. I dreamt that grace a cette ecole, a new conception, was formed entre danseur and artist, avec la musique de Beethoven et de Cesar Franck an ideal in movement, the supreme expression of life.

Just at the moment that I was preparing for the art and the theater, les fetes de la grande joie and human exaltation, other forces were preparing for war, death, and disaster! Alas, I sighed, what are my fallible forces in front of the all powerful ones of war? It seemed natural to give Bellevue for a hospital. Mon Temple de l'art avait ete change en un Royaume de Martyrs of wounded bloody and dying bodies. There, where I dreamed of celestial muses was nothing but sighs of sadness and dispair. Dionysos had completely disappeared. It was the reign of *Christ* after the *Crucifixion*. *My Life*, Isadora Duncan.

Maria Theresa with her sons, Rano and Feodor unknown photographer.

Isadora's Tragic Finale

The beginning of Isadora's tragic descent began on April 19, 1913 at 3:20 P.M. in Paris. While taking a leisurely drive to Versailles, her two little children, Dierdre and Patrick, along with their nurse, were found drowned in the Seine River. The accident was caused by the car stalling due to a taxi that had crossed in front of the car. The driver of the car stepped out to restart the motor without applying the brakes, to prevent the car from rolling into the Seine River, and it disappeared from sight ! The two children were found clinging to their nurse. Patrick had some signs of life and was brought to the American Hospital at Neuilly where the doctors tried to save him. It was Paris Singer who announced to Isadora in a cry, "The children have been killed." This was the trauma that divided Isadora into two people. As she stated, she nearly went out of her mind! She immediately wrote to Gordon Craig telling him that their child Dierdre had been taken from them without speaking, and that no words could express her deep sorrow and pain. He immediately came from Florence where he resided. Paris Singer, who was Patrick's father, was mourning wit Isadora! Her suffering and agony was so intense despite the help and consolation from her friends that she became irrational and experienced extreme states of mental anguish which vascillated between elation and joy, despair and deep depression. Her art was her salvation! She created her most mature and dramatic masterpieces at this time. *The Funeral March* and *Presto* of Chopin, which she created just before the sudden death of the children, was inspired by a strong psychic apparition foretelling of the tragic event. Aside from the subjective interpretation of the piece which was the fear and sadness of losing the children to a death that was unexpected and untimely, and surrender to a fate that was her destiny, the *Presto* symbolized the *spirit* leaving the body after life like the *wind*. The dance has a deeply religious meaning: the Death and Resurrection of Christianity! Isadora said she felt like the crucified Christ; and that some people think their prayers and that she dances hers. During the next fourteen years, she created many new works which where of a *highly spiritual nature*. She said she composed dances inspired entirely by prayer, softness, and light. Walter Rummel was the image of Franz Liszt; tall and thin with an enlarged forehead, and eyes like sources of light, and together they composed pieces to Liszt's -Les Funerailles, Les Pensees de Dieu dan la Solitude, and St. Francis talking to the Birds. "One time again my spirit was revived to life, resurrected by the celestial melodies that sang under his fingers" *(My Life*, 350-351). His was the beginning of the most sacred and pure love of my life. "There was a song by Richard Wagner called L'Ange, where a soul who was sad and desolate visits an angel of light; nobody played Franz Liszt like my archangel, he transported *my soul vers les anges."* Isadora bought a house on *rue de la Pompe,* which was the ancient *salle* Beethoven, where she made her studio. "Under the influence of his love, my dance spiritualized; our two arts united. He initiated me onto the spiritual plane of these works by Franz Liszt. We passed there many hours blessed, our souls transported by the mysterious force that possessed us. As soon as I raised my arms, my soul escaped my body in a long flight. It seemed to me that we had created a spiritual entity distinctly ours, and while the sounds and gestures flew towards infinity another echo responded from above. (*My Life*, p. 354)

My desire to restart my school haunted me until I wired my students in America to come with me to Athens. This turned out to be the stations of my calvary of love, for my Archangel fell for one of my students. I then returned to Paris feeling that both life and love had left me forever; I desired to leave the earth."

In 1921, she received an invitation from the Russian government to come to Russia to open a school. She responded positively to their invitation and asked Maria Theresa, Irma, and the others to accompany her. Maria Theresa said that she refused because she was about to marry Stephen Bourgeois and return to America where she had a career awaiting her. Irma was the only one who assisted Isadora in the foundation of the school in Russia. "Because I was disillusioned, disappointed by my efforts to realize my art in Europe, I was ready to penetrate the Russian ideal. I had not brought one dress with me. I thought I would pass the rest of my life wearing one flannel red blouse amongst friends dressed in equal simplicity filled with fraternal love. *Adieu inegalite,* injustice, and brutality, of the old world that rendered my school impossible." In Moscow she married the famous Russian poet Serge Essenin. After touring together in the United States and Europe they returned to Russia where he took his own life in a hotel room. One more tragedy for Isadora to bear!

She returned to France after a series of disappointing tours as she was mismanaged by theatrical agents until, she settled in Nice to give her last performances and where she herself maintained a studio. With no money in hand and none in sight, her friend Mary Desti paid a visit to Paris Singer, who was spending the summer in his Villa at St. Jean Cap Ferrat. Although he was no longer the millionaire he had been in earlier days (collapse of the Florida land boom had swallowed up an incredible sum in cash and securities), nevertheless he agreed to finance the great artist whom he still admired. (*Russian Days,* p. 362, Irma Duncan). The last program that she was preparing for was the Dante Symphony by Franz Liszt. On Tuesday the 13th of September, Isadora was invited to a dinner at her friend and manager's house, M. Hottois. They were discussing a tour along the Riviera and elsewhere in France. When they brought their child into the room to be presented to Isadora, the smile of the infant was enough to trigger the old wound in her heart. She gave a cry like one hurt to death and ran from the room. She wept all night, and she said "Mary I cannot go on like this; for fourteen years I have had this pain in my heart; I cannot go on, you must find some way for me to end it all. I cannot live in a world where there are beautiful blue–eyed golden haired children. I cannot—I cannot!" After, while dinning together at little restaurant near her studio on the *promenade des anglais.* Mary Desti said: "I feel something terrible is going to happen...please don't go out tonight." her friend said. "I'm going out if it's the last thing I do," said Isadora leaving the restaurant. They returned to the studio, Isadora started the gramophone, and she began to dance to the record that sang out "Bye bye Blackbird": "No one seems to love or understand me, you should hear the stories they all hand me: blackbird bye bye!" As the driver of the Bugatti knocked on the door, Isadora, who had the red woollen shawl draped about her, seized her heavy painted silk shawl, and winding it twice around her neck, danced to the door. As she stood in the doorway ready to go, Mary Desti said, "You had better put on my cloak to keep you warm dear." "No, no I shall be quite warm in my red shawl!" As the driver walked down the path toward the automobile, Isadora danced after him, and as she was about to step in the car, she turned and waved to Mary Desti, calling out. *"Adieu mes amis, je vais a la gloire!"* She the tossed the long fringed end of the shawl over her left shoulder. As the car started forward at full speed, the shawl trailed on the ground beside the wheel. Mary Desti screamed: *"Ton chale, Isadora! Ramasse ton chale!"* The car suddenly stopped. The fringes of the silk shawl and part of the shawl itself were tightly wound round the axel of the wire wheel. The head of Isadora had been pulled down with a sudden jerk as the car had sped forward twenty meters from the studio. Death, which haunted her since April of 1913, finally snatched her with one swift blow and crushed her larynx, broke her neck, and burst her carotid artery. All that could be done to smooth things out was done by Paris Singer, the grief-stricken Lohengrin!

Arrangements were made to have the body brought back to Paris, where it was cremated alongside Dierdre and Patrick her to beloved children. On Friday the sixteenth, the casket containing the body was placed on the Paris bound train and was covered with a rich purple velvet cape that Isadora had always worn when dancing Chopin's "Funeral March" and Liszt's "Les Funerailles"!

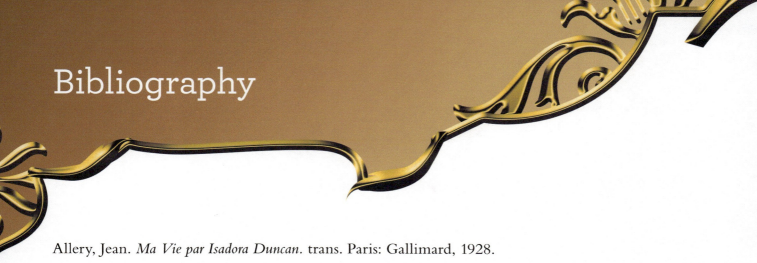

Bibliography

Allery, Jean. *Ma Vie par Isadora Duncan.* trans. Paris: Gallimard, 1928.

Microfiche Biblioteque Nationale, Paris.

Duncan, Isadora. *Ecrit Sur la Danse.* Paris: Ed. Grenier, 1927. Inedits et textes communiquós par. Ch. Dallies, Fernand Divoire, Mario Menuier, George Delaquys, et illustróes de dessins par A. Boudelle, Jose Clara et Grandjouan: Paris, 1927. 85 pp., illus.

Duncan, Isadora. *My Life.* New York: Liveright Publishing Co 1928.

Duncan, Irma and MacDougall, Allan Ross. *Isadora Duncan's Russian Days.* New York: Stratford Press, 1929.

Histoire des Contes et Daufins De Viennois, par Andre Du Chesne Paris, 1628.

Histoire De Dauphine, Du Perier Aymar, Discours Ancien. B.P. in 8.

Histoire De Dauphine et des Princes qui ont porte le nom de Dauphin, Genevre. In-fol 2 Vol.

Holy Spirit, Google Search.

Isadora Duncan. New York: Henry Holt and Company, ed. Paul Magrie, 1947.

Isadora Duncan. Ed. Theatrale, commentary by Auguste Rodin at Trocadero, 1913.

Isadora Duncan, The Danse. New York: Forest Press, 1909.

Isadora Speaks, Isadora Duncan Writings and Speeches, 1981, City Lights Books., San Fransisco

Edited by Franklin Rosemont.

MacDougall, Allan Ross. *Isadora: A Revolutionary in Art and Love.* New York: Thomas Nelson and Sons, 1960.

Making Music for Modern Dance, Edited by Katherine Teck, Oxford Press, Dancing to Beethovens Seventh Symphony.

Seroff, Victor, *The Real Isadora.* New York: The Dial Press.

Videos

Title: *Spiral of Life.* Dances of Isadora Duncan, taught by Maria Theresa Duncan: Chopin-Funeral March and Presto Sonata in B Minor, Op. 35; Franz Liszt- Les Funerailles.

Beethoven's Seventh Symphony, Second Movement, Allegretto A Major, Op. 92. Taught by Maria Theresa Duncan. Filmed at Trianon Palace, Versaille, France

These videos can be seen at the Jerome Robbins Library.

definapamela@yahoo.com
www.facebook.com/pdefina1

Maria Theresa
Divine Being, Guided by a Higher Order

by Pamela De Fina

Maria Theresa, the adopted daughter of the great dancer great Isadora Duncan, shared much in common with her talented and inspirational mother. Maria Theresa was also touched with a talent, a power, a magnificence beyond the limits of most individuals. Theresa was blessed with an intense creativity that compared only to the lengths she would go to share her gift with a young dancer named Pamela De Fina. *Maria Theresa: Divine Being, Guided by a Higher Order* tells the story of Pamela De Fina's ten-year friendship with the great artist Theresa and the inspiration gained from this spiritual coupling of souls and beliefs. The giving and loving nature of Theresa allowed her to share fully with the dancer, the techniques learned at the hands, feet, and soul of Duncan, her mother and mentor, and allows this great Art to live on. Pamela De Fina tells a fascinating, heartfelt, and enrapturing tale in *Maria Theresa: Divine Being, Guided by a Higher Order,* a work those free of heart and enamored of life will be sure to want to share.

Pamela and Maria Theresa at a friend's house, NYC, NY. We were best friends. I was always in awe of her, she was so deep and wise, natural and gentle.

Photo of Maria Theresa Duncan and Pamela De Fina in New York City, around 1985 . This is the studio YWCA on E. 51st, and Lexington ave, NYC where we would practice for 3 hours at a time, 3 days a week, until the choregraphy she taught to me was perfected. The Funeral March and Presto by Chopin, the Allegretto, Beethoven7th symphony, which she referred to as "Your dance, the Light Soul leading the darker shades of the soul towards the light." and Franz Liszts, Les Funerailles, as well as others.of which are eternal treasures, They were of a profoundly spiritual nature, as well as musical., dramatical and artistic. Theresa emphasized making the dances become your own creations, not merely dances to be imitated. As a result I was able to discover my own uniqueness, and she said" The cape is your forte". " It takes a great soul to dance to great music" and "Dear, when you feel deeply, that's life."

Ancient Orchesis Study Group- Director- Prof. Anna Shana, Univ. of Athens, Greece. Presentation on the Anthropological Studies of the Dance. Organized by Professor Anna Shana Ana Sari, and Prof Alkis Raftis, Pres. of Cid- Unesco.

« *Towards an Anthropology of the Dionysian* »

Lecture & Seminar
for the History & Practice of Orchesis
for all

FREE ENTRANCE

& Lecture of Mrs Pamela de Fina
with presentation of documentary
about the personality and influence of Isadora Duncan
http://isadoraduncan.orchesis-portal.org/index.php/ms-
pamela-de-fina

in the context
of the Research meetings of the Ancient Orchesis Study Group of
Dora Stratou Theatre

Thursday, 18 / 5 at 5 – 8 pm
at the House of Dance, In Scholeiou str. no 8 - Plaka

Participation Credit

In the Context
& with the Support of

Mrs. *Pamela De Fina*

contributed to the completion and the celebration
of the publication of the collective volume:

INTERPRETING ANCIENT GREEK DANCE
• WORKBOOKS 2013 – 2018 •

that took place in Athens Cultural Municipality Center
«MELINA»
Irakleidon 66 Thesseion - Keramikos
on **SUNDAY, APRIL 7, 11.30 am**
Organized by the Study Group of "Dora Stratou" Theatre,
with the support of Athens – World Capital of Book of Athens Municipality.

Dr Anna Lazou, assist. prof. of NKUoA
The Book Editor

De Fina

Family Crest, blaison- My Father Major Joseph George De Fina, originally registered Fino da,
Milan, Reipstadt-" Or, Bleu azur, le taut est soumis en demi-pal du meme, avec un dauphin en chef,
nageant naturellement." Larousse Encyclopedia- De Fina- orig.-Provence et aux alentours.

About the Author

Pamela De Fina, Art historian, choreographer, teacher, began her career as an elementary school teacher. As a child she had an innate love of culture, art, music, dance and travel as her name with a dolphin symbolizes - Culture! She was surrounded by beauty, art and beautiful homes, as her Father Major Joseph De Fina entertained an International Society, Ambassadors, World famous tennis players. She studied at Villa Schifanoia, M.A. Art History –Graduate School of Fine Arts/Rosary College, Florence, Italy, and researched High Renaissance Art at Villa I Tatti. She was chosen as a special Protégée of Maria Theresa Duncan and began performing at the United Nations in New York City, in 1979. Pamela has been mentioned in Katherine Teck's book, Oxford Publishing "Making Music for Modern Dance," for performing the Beethoven's Symphony 7 in A Major- Allegretto, filmed at the Trianon Palace, Versailles, taught by Maria Theresa Duncan. She has revealed an inter–disciplinary approach to the Arts.

She has produced videos, Maria Theresa and the Classical Dance,"The Spiral of Life," and Beethoven 7 Symphony, Allegretto", "Concert at the House of the Redeemer". She has lectured on the "Parallels between works of Art, Renaissance, Greek and Roman, and the Dance," at San Marino World Congress on Dance Research cid-Unesco, Isadora and La Belle Epoch, a book entitled, "Maria Theresa Divine Being Guided by a Higher Order," written and published at Female Artists in History -Facebook. Paris Womens Journal- She has performed and lectured at the Sorbonne University, Paris France, Graymoor Fransiscan Friary, Norton Museum WPB, Fl, Lannan Museum, Centre de Danse du Marais, Paris, and Santa Barbara City College Abroad in Paris France, the Society of the Four Arts, George Washington Univ, and the Univ. of Athens Greece, Ancient Orchesis .study group in Athens, Greece. Pen Ladies International, Palm Beach Yacht Club, and is a member of CID-UNESCO. She began dancing when she was 5 at Imperial Studios, Palm Beach, Fl, under the direction of Joanna Kneeland, and performed with famous ballerinas at the Palm Beach Playhouse, and was offered a scholarship to study ballet at the Harkness House in NYC. I chose instead a life of education, culture, art and travel. Later, I returned to the Harkness House of Ballet in NYC.

She received a BA EL. ED, and Art History, and taught 5th grade for a few years before marrying an internationally acclaimed artist. living and studying, in Santa Barbara, Ca, where she attended UCSB, Art History, and in Florence, Italy at the Graduate school of Fine Arts/Rosary College in Florence Italy, MA Art History program.